HENRY BLACKABY

Reflections on the Seven Realities

of Experiencing God

HENRY BLACKABY

Reflections on the Seven Realities

of Experiencing God

Nashville, Tennessee

Reflections on the Seven Realities
of Experiencing God

CONTENTS

INTRODUCTION

Experiencing God is so much more than just a Bible study course. It is truly a way of life, a daily adventure for those who decide to take seriously their relationship with the Father and their place in this world.

Surely, it is this fact—that we can experience God in the here and now—that transports our Christian lives beyond cold, tasteless ritual and into the surging, exhilarating flow of God's eternal activity.

This book is an invitation for you to enlarge your view of God, to embrace the love He has for you, and to embark on a lifelong journey of following Him...wherever He desires to take you.

It is the only life that is really worth living.

For when God awakens in you a thirst for spiritual things, nothing else can satisfy your hunger for meaning and purpose but a real-life encounter with the living God. As the Holy Spirit speaks to you through the thoughts and Scriptures in this book, He will be drawing you to a life beyond anything you have ever known, a life so dependent on the direction of God that you will no longer find fulfillment in pursuing your own plans.

Are you ready for God to use you for His higher purposes, to surround you with other believers who are also experiencing His stirring in their souls, and to make your daily life a living witness to the power of God?

Then open your heart to what God has to say. Submit your dreams and ambitions to the One who made you. And begin following Him into the corners of your world where He has work to do—and you to do it with.

Come experience God!

"This is eternal life:
that they may know You,
the only true God,
and the One You have sent—
Jesus Christ."

—John 17:3

Reality #1
GOD IS ALWAYS AT WORK AROUND YOU

*"My Father is still working,
and I also am working."*
—John 5:17

God has not left the world to function on its own. He has been actively involved throughout history, orchestrating time and events, doing what only God can do—seeking and saving that which is lost.

The Bible says that no one desires to follow God on their own, that only God can draw people to Himself. So when you see these things happening around you—when people are asking questions and wanting to talk about spiritual things—you can be sure that God is at work.

And you can be sure that He has placed you right in the middle of His will.

GOD IS ALWAYS AT WORK AROUND YOU

Always assume that God is at work. When He reveals a spiritual truth to you (another thing that only God can do), do not simply treat it as a devotional thought to make you feel better through the day.

Ask Him to help you take what you are hearing and connect it with what you see happening around you. Immediately look to see what He wants you to do with what He has said.

Once you join God in what He is doing, you will experience Him accomplishing His activity through your life—in ways you have never known before.

"*The words I speak to you*
I do not speak on My own.
The Father who lives in Me does His works."

—John 14:10

Jesus always knew what to do throughout His life, because He was always looking to see what the Father was doing. Whatever the Father did, the Son did. If Christ Himself was that dependent on the Father, think how dependent we should be on God the Father working in and through us.

GOD IS ALWAYS AT WORK AROUND YOU

ANTICIPATE
that God will start working with you.

God usually came to people in the Scriptures right in the middle of their ordinary routine, right as they were doing the last thing they knew to do. You do not need to be doing anything special for God to use you. Simply be willing to submit to Him at any time, at a moment's notice.

God has used Henry to remind me
of this truth: It's better to be still and
do nothing _with_ God than to be busy
and do much _without_ Him.

—Max Lucado

GOD IS ALWAYS AT WORK AROUND YOU

You never find God asking people to dream up what they want to do for Him. The pattern in the Scripture looks like this: You submit yourself to God, and you wait until He shows you what He is about to do.

For unless God allows you to see where He is working, you will not see it. You can involve yourself in doing good things, but you may miss the work that God intended you to do.

The servant doesn't tell the Master what kind of assignment he needs. Instead, he waits on his Master to give him the assignment.

MAKE IT YOUR REALITY

Can you identify times when God was at work around you—and you knew it? Or looking back, can you think of times when God was working around you, but you didn't recognize it?

Invite God to initiate His work in you any time He chooses. Start by loving Him, and then be listening for Him.

"What can we do to perform the works of God?" they asked.
Jesus replied, "This is the work of God:
that you believe in the One He has sent."

—John 6:28-29

Reality #2

GOD PURSUES A LOVE RELATIONSHIP WITH YOU

Love consists in this: not that we loved God,
but that He loved us and sent His Son.
—1 John 4:10

Do you realize that God determined to love you? When you were not His friend, He drew you with cords of love. When you were still His enemy, He gave His own Son to die for you. Is there any greater expression of love than this?

You should never look at anything that happens in your life without seeing it against the backdrop of the cross, where God proved once and for all just how much He loves you.

In order to experience God and know His will, you must be absolutely convinced of His love for you.

GOD PURSUES A LOVE RELATIONSHIP WITH YOU

The Scripture leads us to understand that God is saying, "I want you to love Me above everything else. When you are in a relationship of love with Me, you have everything there is."

Everything in your Christian life, everything about knowing and experiencing God, everything about understanding His will depends on the quality of your love relationship with God. If that is not right, nothing else will be right.

To be loved by God is the highest relationship, the highest achievement, and the highest position in life.

The one who does not love does not know God,
because God is love.
—1 John 4:8

God's very nature is love. Therefore, He will never express Himself to His children in any way other than perfect love. Even His discipline is an act of love, for in conforming us to the image of His Son, God is enabling us to experience Him at work in our lives.

GOD PURSUES A LOVE RELATIONSHIP WITH YOU

If you want God to be real to you,

LOVE HIM.

The one thing God wants from you is to love Him. Yes, God will call you to obey Him and to do whatever He asks of you. But you do not need to be doing something to be fulfilled. You are fulfilled completely in your relationship with God. When you are filled with Him, what else do you need?

All seven realities are critical, but I, such an undeserving ragamuffin, am so grateful that God desires to have a love relationship with me. I still cannot fathom that He loves me with a completely unfailing, unchanging love—no matter how I disappoint myself or anyone else. I grieve for people who only see the Word of God as a volume of endless rules and regulations. The Bible is a love story! Sure, it has do's and don'ts, but each one is for the purpose of enhancing the most sacred romance mortal creatures could ever imagine! One cannot possibly experience God and not experience love divine... all love's excelling.

—Beth Moore

GOD PURSUES A LOVE RELATIONSHIP WITH YOU

Perhaps you struggle to obey God or to consistently have time alone with Him. If that is a problem you face, make it a priority in your life to love Him with all your heart. Obedience problems are really love problems.

Try not to think of the time you spend with God as a duty. The purpose of a quiet time is for you to get to know God. And as you come to know Him, you can walk out of your special times with God enjoying a living relationship with Him that you can cultivate all day long—throughout all your life.

Make It Your Reality

Can you describe your relationship with God by sincerely saying, "I love Him with all my heart"?

Go before the Lord and ask Him to open your eyes to the love He has for you. When you love Him as you should, you will always be in fellowship with the Father.

"If anyone loves Me, he will keep My word. My Father will love him, and We will come to him and make Our home with him."

—John 14:23

Reality #3

GOD INVITES YOU TO JOIN HIM IN HIS WORK

It is God who is working among you...
for His good purpose.
—Philippians 2:13

When God was ready to judge the world with a flood, He came to Noah. When He desired to build a nation for Himself, He turned to Abraham. When He heard His children groaning under Egyptian bondage, He appeared in a burning bush to Moses.

They were three of the most ordinary of men. But God had work to do, and He knew just who to do it with.

God has always given His people assignments that are too big for them to handle alone, so that a watching world can see—not what *we* can do—but what *God* can do.

GOD INVITES YOU TO JOIN HIM IN HIS WORK

The call to salvation is at the same time a call to be on mission with God. These are not separate callings but are all part of the same experience.

You cannot be drawn into relationship with God without also having the heart of God laid over your heart—without wanting to put your life alongside His and join Him in doing His will.

Yet we are often so self-centered. Love for God demands that we constantly shift our hearts away from what *we* want in order to hear and desire what *God* wants.

"Well done, good and faithful slave!
You were faithful over a few things;
I will put you in charge of many things."
—*Matthew 25:21*

When God is ready, He will show you where He is working so you can join Him. But He usually starts small and builds character to match each assignment. Don't get discouraged if God's call doesn't come immediately. Wait on Him and keep watching. He knows what He is doing.

Have open ears,
a willing heart, and a ready
"YES."

God wants to touch people in your community. Suppose He wants to do it through you. But you give Him a whole list of reasons why you can't. Any assignment that comes from God will be more than you can handle. It will always have a God-sized dimension to it.

Whenever I enter a contract with anyone, they usually ask me to sign on the bottom line. What that usually means is that I have agreed to the terms and conditions of the contract. Like the contractor, we too often give God a full page of activities we are going to do for Him and ask Him to sign off on it. Instead, God gives us a blank sheet of paper for us to sign on the bottom line, demonstrating our trust in Him and His will for our lives. The question is not "Will God sign off on what we want to do?" but rather "Will we trust God to do what He wants done?"

—Tony Evans

GOD INVITES YOU TO JOIN HIM IN HIS WORK

To get some idea of the kind of assignments you can expect from God, make note of those moments in your life when God did something unique, when you had a significant experience with Him, when you could have turned one way but He took you another.

God usually builds on what He has already done. So if you can determine the consistent patterns God has used to direct and redirect you throughout your life, you can be pretty sure that He will continue to lead you down the path He has begun. These experiences are not ends in themselves but opportunities for you to trust Him further.

Make It Your Reality

Do you love God enough—are you thankful enough for His gift of salvation—to join Him in reaching out to a hurting world, to be willing for Him to take you beyond the limits of your own abilities?

Then be ready for God to reveal your next assignment. Be ready when He says to go.

May the God of peace...equip you with all that is good to do His will, working in us what is pleasing in His sight.
—Hebrews 13:20-21

GOD SPEAKS
TO HIS PEOPLE

My sheep hear My voice,
I know them, and they follow Me.
—John 10:27

If there is one truth you see on nearly every page of the Scriptures, it is this: God speaks to His people. From Adam in the Garden, to John on the island of Patmos, from Genesis to Revelation, God is speaking where His people can hear Him.

Why is that so hard to believe? If you were going somewhere with a friend, would you expect him to walk silently beside you, never saying a word? So if you are walking with God, shouldn't you expect Him to want to share with you what is on His heart?

Don't good fathers talk to their children?

GOD SPEAKS TO HIS PEOPLE

The key to knowing God's voice is not a formula or a method you can follow. Knowing God's voice comes from an intimate love relationship with Him. You come to know His voice as you experience His presence.

As you relate to God on a daily basis, the Spirit of God takes the Word of God, couples it with the will of God, and helps you to understand the ways of God.

God's main reason for speaking to you is to reveal and clarify who He is, because the more you know about Him, the more you know how to follow Him.

We also speak these things,
not in words taught by human wisdom,
but in those taught by the Spirit,
explaining spiritual things to spiritual people.
—1 Corinthians 2:13

Throughout your life, you will experience times when you want to respond to a situation based on your own experiences or wisdom. This should be your guideline: Always go back to the Bible, and ask the Holy Spirit to reveal truth to you.

GOD SPEAKS TO HIS PEOPLE

LISTEN,
and God will speak where you can hear.

When you pray, never let it cross your mind that God is not going to answer. Sometimes He is silent as He prepares to bring you into a deeper understanding of Himself. But whenever a silence comes, continue obeying all you know to do, and watch and wait for a fresh encounter with Him.

To hear God speak, we must first determine to listen for the voice of God. We reveal that determination by our willingness to obey His voice—no matter what He might say. And we illustrate our willingness to obey God's voice by our present obedience to what He has already declared so clearly in His Word. This "obedience factor" prepares us to hear God's voice in our present day experience. Henry has taught us to look at everyday events and ask the questions: "What is God doing through these events?" and "What is He saying to me?" My wife, Paula, and I have walked in the firm assurance that God speaks clearly to His children.

—Ken Hemphill

GOD SPEAKS TO HIS PEOPLE

God speaks through the Scripture, through prayer, through circumstances, and through His people. Look for God to be speaking in all these ways, because walking with Him involves relating to Him in every aspect of your life.

When what you are hearing in all these areas continues lining up to say the same thing, then you know that you need to start moving in that direction.

Circumstances can be confusing at times, but God can help you interpret them from His perspective, letting you see how He is working through them in order to accomplish His will.

Make It Your Reality

God reveals His plans so that He can accomplish His work through you in such a way that He gets all the glory.

So ask God to help you know when He is speaking, to know what He is saying, and to know how to respond in obedience. Listen for Him, and learn of Him.

"When the Spirit of truth comes,
He will guide you into all the truth....
He will speak whatever He hears."
—John 16:13

GOD'S INVITATION LEADS TO A CRISIS OF BELIEF

*Without faith it is
impossible to please God.*
—Hebrews 11:6

When God speaks, He requires two things of us—faith and action. But because we tend to want to think for ourselves and go at our own pace, God's invitation sets up a conflict in our lives.

In situations like these, we face a crisis of belief—when God tests us to see if He has our heart at His control. For the way we respond to an assignment from God will reveal how much we really love Him, regardless of what we say.

When God speaks, that *is* the experience with Him. When God calls, *that moment* is the time to act.

GOD'S INVITATION LEADS TO A CRISIS OF BELIEF

Many people get an assignment from God and say, "That couldn't possibly be from God. That's not the area of my gifts." But often our natural abilities stand in the way of what God desires to accomplish through us.

We forget that when God speaks, He reveals what He has already determined to do—not what He wants us to do for Him.

Only God can tell you what He wants to do through your life. You will not be able to figure that out on your own. *He knows* that you can't do it! He wants to do it Himself—*through* you.

Jesus said, "With men it is impossible,
but not with God,
because all things are possible with God."
—Mark 10:27

If you know that God is calling you, step out in faith—even if the money is not in hand, even if the people are not in place, even if the end is not in sight. God never calls you accidentally or incidentally, but always with a clear purpose in mind for your life.

GOD'S INVITATION LEADS TO A CRISIS OF BELIEF

LET FAITH
lead you where logic cannot go.

One sure way to grow in your relationship with God is to promise you will accept the next assignment He gives you, because it will almost always be greater than the previous one. Each assignment is a moment of truth, an opportunity to increase your capacity of faith.

One of the greatest difficulties of hearing God is the fact that often what He says is what we do not want to hear. "Forgive that person you hate," He whispers. Or "Give up what is most precious to you." And so while we are doing the impossible (listening to the silence of prayer) He often asks the impossible of us. But Jesus has said that all things are possible for God, even speaking to ears that are deaf to Him and commanding those of us who are dead in our sin to live, move, and have our being.

—Michael Card

GOD'S INVITATION LEADS TO A CRISIS OF BELIEF

Mature believers never outgrow the experience of being scared half to death by the assignments God gives them. But that is His loving way of leading you closer to Him—always putting your next assignment just out of reach, requiring a dimension of faith that lies just beyond the last point of your trusting.

The kind of assignments God gives are always beyond what people can do because He wants to demonstrate His nature, His strength, His provision, and His kindness—through you to those He is drawing to Himself.

Make It Your Reality

Two words you should never use in the same sentence are these: "No, Lord."

God's assignments are not ideas for you to think about or questions for you to meditate on for six weeks. They are directives from the Maker of all things. They are instructions for you to obey.

"When you have done all that you were commanded, you should say, 'We are good-for-nothing slaves; we've only done our duty.' "

—Luke 17:10

Reality #6
JOINING GOD REQUIRES MAJOR ADJUSTMENTS

"No one can be a slave of two masters."
—Matthew 6:24

The first few realities of experiencing God are truths that most any believer finds warm and comforting. But these last two or three realities are where the way becomes narrow—where God is speaking, but where faith is inconvenient.

You cannot continue life as usual and expect God to use you. You cannot stay where you are and go with God at the same time.

When God invites you to join Him, the first action will involve the adjustment of your life to God and His ways. The second action will be obedience. But you cannot go on to obedience without first making the adjustments.

Joining God requires major adjustments

The reality of adjusting to God holds true throughout Scripture. David could not continue herding sheep on the hillsides and become king of Israel. Jonah had to overcome a major prejudice in order to preach to the people of Ninevah. Peter and others had to leave their fishing businesses in order to follow Jesus.

Obeying God will always come at a cost. But few people take into account the cost of *not* obeying God. It is always much higher.

God can do in six months through a life adjusted to Him what He cannot do in six years through those who choose to follow their own way.

*"Whoever does not bear his own cross
and come after Me cannot be My disciple."*

—*Luke 14:27*

We tend to orchestrate ourselves into a comfort zone. We want gifts that agree with us, a ministry we can handle, a job that is secure, a way that is familiar. But when God speaks, He constantly upsets our plans for comfortable living. He graciously provides us the tension we need to step out in faith.

It's time to

FOLLOW GOD
for a change.

The main adjustment you must make in becoming a disciple is to stop doing work *for* God according to *your* abilities, *your* likes, *your* goals, on *your* timetable, and begin living in total dependence on God and *His* working, resources, and timing. This is a major adjustment, and it is never easy to make.

In 1998, Henry Blackaby came to Promise Keepers to speak to our staff. Prior to coming, he had asked God if He had a word for us. As Henry searched the Gospels to see if the Holy Spirit would move, Luke 23:26 jumped off the pages: "They seized Simon, a Cyrenian, who was coming in from the country, and laid the cross on him to carry behind Jesus." Henry explained that God had called me out of coaching and had given the cross of racial-denominational reconciliation to Promise Keepers. "Carry it faithfully," he said. I received this word and carry it in my heart today.

—Bill McCartney

JOINING GOD REQUIRES MAJOR ADJUSTMENTS

Adjusting to God is a daily experience, but be careful not to think He always wants you to immediately do something rash or drastic. Often, God is alerting you to what He is *about* to do, inviting you to begin the process of getting your life in order for Him to use you.

He may require you to make adjustments in your circumstances (your job, for example), your relationships, your thinking, your commitments, your actions, or your beliefs.

He will help you know what you should do at each point along the way, but you must choose to make the adjustments.

Make It Your Reality

What's holding you back from giving God everything? A certain sin or a lazy habit? Your friends' opinions? Your current career path?

Who knows what waits just over the next sunrise if you are willing to surrender your whole life—all of it—to the Lordship of Christ?

I have been crucified with Christ;
and I no longer live, but Christ lives in me...
who loved me and gave Himself for me.
—Galatians 2:19-20

Reality #7
YOU EXPERIENCE GOD
AS YOU OBEY HIM

He who calls you is faithful,
who also will do it.
—1 Thessalonians 5:24

You can know about God as Provider when you read of the time God provided a ram for Abraham to sacrifice in place of his son, Isaac. But you *really* know God as Provider when you experience Him providing something in *your life*.

You can know about God as being a Banner when you read of Moses holding up his hands, giving constant glory to God as he overlooked the battle with the Amalekites. But you know God as *your* Banner when He delivers you from a battle in your own life.

To know Him is to experience Him.

YOU EXPERIENCE GOD AS YOU OBEY HIM

Deep experiences with God immediately follow your first step of obedience. Unless you do what God has clearly instructed you to do, you will wonder why others continue to grow while you continue to struggle.

The children of Israel discovered this when God told them He would part the waters of the Jordan before them when the priests carrying the Ark of the Covenant put their feet into the water. They did, and God led them safely across.

We would prefer Him to part the water before we take a step into the unknown, but obedience to God is what unlocks the experience of His power.

Whoever keeps His word,
truly in him the love of God is perfected.
This is how we know we are in Him.

—1 John 2:5

The pattern of experiencing God is to daily surrender your life to His life, and your will to His will, letting God be God—unconditionally—on His own terms. Just as Jesus "learned obedience through what He suffered," we must learn obedience by yielding ourselves to Him each day.

ODEDIENCE
will point you in the ways of God.

As you do the next thing God tells you, you are allowing Him to place you into the mighty, sweeping movement of God. You are opening yourself to possibilities far beyond anything your mind could conceive. You are joining Him in what He is doing, and discovering your place in the living body of Christ.

Authentic faith—the kind that evokes extreme reactions from those it touches—is a faith characterized by faithfulness in both word and deed. It's not blind faith. Real faith is illuminating. It creates courage in the coward to stand fast on the promises of God, even in the presence of the threats of men. It's not always in the cloak of outwardly religious words and worship. It's based on our relationship to Jesus Christ, and it results in obedience to His commands. Experiencing God is the result of authentic faith.

—Gov. Mike Huckabee

YOU EXPERIENCE GOD AS YOU OBEY HIM

Jesus never failed to know and do the will of His Father. Every solitary thing the Father wanted to do through Him, Jesus did it immediately.

Yes, we all are a long way from Christ's perfect example. But the Christ who lived His life in complete obedience is fully present in us. And He will never fail to pull our lives into the middle of His purpose.

If you walk in a consistent relationship with God, you should never experience a time when you do not know the will of God and are enabled by Him to carry it out.

MAKE IT YOUR REALITY

Would you like to go with God into the deepest experience you have ever known with Him?

Agree with God in prayer that anything He asks of you is reasonable. And begin watching for Him to test the sincerity of your commitment. He longs for you to experience Him. Do you?

"Everyone who hears these words of Mine
and acts on them will be like a sensible man
who built his house on the rock."

—Matthew 7:24

I am sure of this,
that He who started a good work in you
will carry it on to completion
until the day of Christ Jesus.

—Philippians 1:6

List of Illustrations:

Acknowledgements

Thank you to those who contributed your thoughts
and insights to this book. Your help, your wisdom,
and your generosity are greatly appreciated.

Max Lucado

Beth Moore

Tony Evans

Ken Hemphill

Michael Card

Bill McCartney

Mike Huckabee

The enclosed CD features five full-length selections from *Experiencing God...The Musical*, a worshipful, 70-minute presentation on knowing and doing the will of God, written by Gary Rhodes and Claire Cloninger.

For more information on this inspiring Genevox musical, call 1-800-436-3869. Promo Paks—which include one choral book and a complete CD or cassette recording—are available now (limit one per church).

CD Promo Pak 0-6330-0722-6

Cassette Promo Pak 0-6330-0721-8